Storyboard 16:9 Notebook

120 Pages to Assist the Creative Process

_____

_____

_____

Prodigious Preproduction Planning Prevents
Piss-Poor Postproduction.

- Robert Petrie

Title: _____   Date: _____

Scene:	Shot:	No.

Scene:	Shot:	No.

Scene:	Shot:	No.

Scene:	Shot:	No.

Title: _____   Date: _____

Scene:	Shot:	No.

Scene:	Shot:	No.

Scene:	Shot:	No.

Scene:	Shot:	No.

Title: _____   Date: _____

Scene:	Shot:	No.

_____

_____

_____

_____

_____

_____

Scene:	Shot:	No.

_____

_____

_____

_____

_____

_____

Scene:	Shot:	No.

_____

_____

_____

_____

_____

_____

Scene:	Shot:	No.

_____

_____

_____

_____

_____

_____

Title: _____ Date: _____

Scene:	Shot:	No.

Scene:	Shot:	No.

Scene:	Shot:	No.

Scene:	Shot:	No.

Title: _____   Date: _____

Scene:	Shot:	No.

Scene:	Shot:	No.

Scene:	Shot:	No.

Scene:	Shot:	No.

Title: _____   Date: _____

Scene:	Shot:	No.

Scene:	Shot:	No.

Scene:	Shot:	No.

Scene:	Shot:	No.

Title: _____   Date: _____

Scene:	Shot:	No.

Scene:	Shot:	No.

Scene:	Shot:	No.

Scene:	Shot:	No.

Title: _____   Date: _____

Scene:	Shot:	No.

Scene:	Shot:	No.

Scene:	Shot:	No.

Scene:	Shot:	No.

10

Title: _____   Date: _____

Scene:	Shot:	No.

Scene:	Shot:	No.

Scene:	Shot:	No.

Scene:	Shot:	No.

Title: _____   Date: _____

Scene:	Shot:	No.

Scene:	Shot:	No.

Scene:	Shot:	No.

Scene:	Shot:	No.

Title: _____   Date: _____

Scene:	Shot:	No.

Scene:	Shot:	No.

Scene:	Shot:	No.

Scene:	Shot:	No.

Title: _____   Date: _____

Scene:	Shot:	No.

_____

_____

_____

_____

_____

_____

Scene:	Shot:	No.

_____

_____

_____

_____

_____

_____

Scene:	Shot:	No.

_____

_____

_____

_____

_____

_____

Scene:	Shot:	No.

_____

_____

_____

_____

_____

_____

Title: _____   Date: _____

Scene:	Shot:	No.

_____

_____

_____

_____

_____

_____

_____

Scene:	Shot:	No.

_____

_____

_____

_____

_____

_____

_____

Scene:	Shot:	No.

_____

_____

_____

_____

_____

_____

_____

Scene:	Shot:	No.

_____

_____

_____

_____

_____

_____

_____

Title: _____   Date: _____

Scene:	Shot:	No.

Scene:	Shot:	No.

Scene:	Shot:	No.

Scene:	Shot:	No.

16

Title: _____   Date: _____

Scene:	Shot:	No.

Scene:	Shot:	No.

Scene:	Shot:	No.

Scene:	Shot:	No.

Title: _____   Date: _____

Scene:	Shot:	No.

Scene:	Shot:	No.

Scene:	Shot:	No.

Scene:	Shot:	No.

18

Title: _____   Date: _____

Scene:	Shot:	No.

Scene:	Shot:	No.

Scene:	Shot:	No.

Scene:	Shot:	No.

Title: _____   Date: _____

Scene:	Shot:	No.

Scene:	Shot:	No.

Scene:	Shot:	No.

Scene:	Shot:	No.

20

Title: _____   Date: _____

Scene:	Shot:	No.

Scene:	Shot:	No.

Scene:	Shot:	No.

Scene:	Shot:	No.

Title: _____   Date: _____

Scene:	Shot:	No.

Scene:	Shot:	No.

Scene:	Shot:	No.

Scene:	Shot:	No.

Title: _____   Date: _____

Scene:	Shot:	No.

_____

_____

_____

_____

_____

_____

Scene:	Shot:	No.

_____

_____

_____

_____

_____

_____

Scene:	Shot:	No.

_____

_____

_____

_____

_____

_____

Scene:	Shot:	No.

_____

_____

_____

_____

_____

_____

Title: _____   Date: _____

Scene:	Shot:	No.

Scene:	Shot:	No.

Scene:	Shot:	No.

Scene:	Shot:	No.

24

Title: _____   Date: _____

Scene:	Shot:	No.

Scene:	Shot:	No.

Scene:	Shot:	No.

Scene:	Shot:	No.

Title: _____   Date: _____

25

Scene:	Shot:	No.

Scene:	Shot:	No.

Scene:	Shot:	No.

Scene:	Shot:	No.

Title: _____ Date: _____

Scene:	Shot:	No.

Scene:	Shot:	No.

Scene:	Shot:	No.

Scene:	Shot:	No.

Title: _____   Date: _____

Scene:	Shot:	No.

_____

_____

_____

_____

_____

_____

Scene:	Shot:	No.

_____

_____

_____

_____

_____

Scene:	Shot:	No.

_____

_____

_____

_____

_____

_____

Scene:	Shot:	No.

_____

_____

_____

_____

_____

Title: _____   Date: _____

Scene:	Shot:	No.

Scene:	Shot:	No.

Scene:	Shot:	No.

Scene:	Shot:	No.

Title: _____   Date: _____

Scene:	Shot:	No.

Scene:	Shot:	No.

Scene:	Shot:	No.

Scene:	Shot:	No.

Title: _____   Date: _____

Scene: _____   Shot: _____   No. _____

Scene: _____   Shot: _____   No. _____

Scene: _____   Shot: _____   No. _____

Scene: _____   Shot: _____   No. _____

Title: _____   Date: _____

Scene: _____ Shot: _____ No. _____

Scene: _____ Shot: _____ No. _____

Scene: _____ Shot: _____ No. _____

Scene: _____ Shot: _____ No. _____

Title: _____   Date: _____

Scene: Shot: No.

Scene: Shot: No.

Scene: Shot: No.

Scene: Shot: No.

Title: _____ Date: _____

Scene: _____ Shot: _____ No. _____

Scene: _____ Shot: _____ No. _____

Scene: _____ Shot: _____ No. _____

Scene: _____ Shot: _____ No. _____

34

Title: _____   Date: _____

Scene: _____ Shot: _____ No. _____

Scene: _____ Shot: _____ No. _____

Scene: _____ Shot: _____ No. _____

Scene: _____ Shot: _____ No. _____

Title: _____   Date: _____

Scene:	Shot:	No.

Scene:	Shot:	No.

Scene:	Shot:	No.

Scene:	Shot:	No.

36

Title: _____   Date: _____

Scene:	Shot:	No.

Scene:	Shot:	No.

Scene:	Shot:	No.

Scene:	Shot:	No.

Title: _____   Date: _____

Scene: _____ Shot: _____ No. _____

Scene: _____ Shot: _____ No. _____

Scene: _____ Shot: _____ No. _____

Scene: _____ Shot: _____ No. _____

Title: _____   Date: _____

Scene: Shot: No.

Scene: Shot: No.

Scene: Shot: No.

Scene: Shot: No.

Title: _____   Date: _____

Scene:	Shot:	No.

Scene:	Shot:	No.

Scene:	Shot:	No.

Scene:	Shot:	No.

Title: _____   Date: _____

Scene:	Shot:	No.

Scene:	Shot:	No.

Scene:	Shot:	No.

Scene:	Shot:	No.

Title: _____   Date: _____

Scene: _____ Shot: _____ No.

Scene: _____ Shot: _____ No.

Scene: _____ Shot: _____ No.

Scene: _____ Shot: _____ No.

Title: _____ Date: _____

Scene:	Shot:	No.

Scene:	Shot:	No.

Scene:	Shot:	No.

Scene:	Shot:	No.

Title: _____   Date: _____

Scene:	Shot:	No.

Scene:	Shot:	No.

Scene:	Shot:	No.

Scene:	Shot:	No.

44

Title: _____   Date: _____

Scene: _____ Shot: _____ No. _____

Scene: _____ Shot: _____ No. _____

Scene: _____ Shot: _____ No. _____

Scene: _____ Shot: _____ No. _____

Title: _____   Date: _____

Scene:	Shot:	No.

Scene:	Shot:	No.

Scene:	Shot:	No.

Scene:	Shot:	No.

Title: _____ Date: _____

| Scene: | Shot: | No. |

| Scene: | Shot: | No. |

| Scene: | Shot: | No. |

| Scene: | Shot: | No. |

Title: _____   Date: _____

Scene:	Shot:	No.

Scene:	Shot:	No.

Scene:	Shot:	No.

Scene:	Shot:	No.

48

Title: _____   Date: _____

Scene: Shot: No.

Scene: Shot: No.

Scene: Shot: No.

Scene: Shot: No.

Title: _____   Date: _____

Scene:	Shot:	No.

Scene:	Shot:	No.

Scene:	Shot:	No.

Scene:	Shot:	No.

Title: _____   Date: _____

Scene: _____ Shot: _____ No. _____

Scene: _____ Shot: _____ No. _____

Scene: _____ Shot: _____ No. _____

Scene: _____ Shot: _____ No. _____

Title: _____   Date: _____

51

_____

_____

_____

_____

_____

Scene:	Shot:	No.

_____

_____

_____

_____

_____

Scene:	Shot:	No.

_____

_____

_____

_____

_____

Scene:	Shot:	No.

_____

_____

_____

_____

_____

Scene:	Shot:	No.

52

Title: _____   Date: _____

Scene:	Shot:	No.

Scene:	Shot:	No.

Scene:	Shot:	No.

Scene:	Shot:	No.

Title: _____   Date: _____

Scene: Shot: No.

Scene: Shot: No.

Scene: Shot: No.

Scene: Shot: No.

Title: _____   Date: _____

Scene:	Shot:	No.

Scene:	Shot:	No.

Scene:	Shot:	No.

Scene:	Shot:	No.

55

Title: _____   Date: _____

Scene:	Shot:	No.

Scene:	Shot:	No.

Scene:	Shot:	No.

Scene:	Shot:	No.

Title: _____ Date: _____

Scene:	Shot:	No.

Scene:	Shot:	No.

Scene:	Shot:	No.

Scene:	Shot:	No.

Title: _____   Date: _____

Scene:	Shot:	No.

_____

_____

_____

_____

_____

_____

Scene:	Shot:	No.

_____

_____

_____

_____

_____

_____

Scene:	Shot:	No.

_____

_____

_____

_____

_____

_____

Scene:	Shot:	No.

_____

_____

_____

_____

_____

_____

Title: _____ Date: _____

| Scene: | Shot: | No. |

| Scene: | Shot: | No. |

| Scene: | Shot: | No. |

| Scene: | Shot: | No. |

Title: _____   Date: _____

Scene:	Shot:	No.

Scene:	Shot:	No.

Scene:	Shot:	No.

Scene:	Shot:	No.

Title: _____   Date: _____

Scene:	Shot:	No.

Scene:	Shot:	No.

Scene:	Shot:	No.

Scene:	Shot:	No.

Title: _____   Date: _____

Scene: Shot: No.

Scene: Shot: No.

Scene: Shot: No.

Scene: Shot: No.

Title: _____ Date: _____

Scene: Shot: No.

Scene: Shot: No.

Scene: Shot: No.

Scene: Shot: No.

Title: _____   Date: _____

Scene: _____   Shot: _____   No.

_____

_____

_____

_____

_____

_____

Scene: _____   Shot: _____   No.

_____

_____

_____

_____

_____

_____

Scene: _____   Shot: _____   No.

_____

_____

_____

_____

_____

_____

Scene: _____   Shot: _____   No.

_____

_____

_____

_____

_____

_____

64

Title: _____   Date: _____

Scene:	Shot:	No.

Scene:	Shot:	No.

Scene:	Shot:	No.

Scene:	Shot:	No.

Title: _____   Date: _____

Scene: _____ Shot: _____ No. _____

_____

_____

_____

_____

_____

_____

Scene: _____ Shot: _____ No. _____

_____

_____

_____

_____

_____

_____

Scene: _____ Shot: _____ No. _____

_____

_____

_____

_____

_____

Scene: _____ Shot: _____ No. _____

_____

_____

_____

_____

_____

_____

Title: _____   Date: _____

Scene: Shot: No.

Scene: Shot: No.

Scene: Shot: No.

Scene: Shot: No.

Title: _____   Date: _____

Scene:	Shot:	No.

Scene:	Shot:	No.

Scene:	Shot:	No.

Scene:	Shot:	No.

68

Title: _____   Date: _____

Scene: Shot: No.

Scene: Shot: No.

Scene: Shot: No.

Scene: Shot: No.

Title: _____   Date: _____

Scene: Shot: No.

Scene: Shot: No.

Scene: Shot: No.

Scene: Shot: No.

70

Title: _____   Date: _____

Scene: Shot: No.

Scene: Shot: No.

Scene: Shot: No.

Scene: Shot: No.

Title: _____   Date: _____

Scene:	Shot:	No.

Scene:	Shot:	No.

Scene:	Shot:	No.

Scene:	Shot:	No.

72

Title: _____   Date: _____

Scene:	Shot:	No.

Scene:	Shot:	No.

Scene:	Shot:	No.

Scene:	Shot:	No.

Title: _____   Date: _____

Scene:	Shot:	No.

Scene:	Shot:	No.

Scene:	Shot:	No.

Scene:	Shot:	No.

Title: _____   Date: _____

Scene: _____ Shot: _____ No. _____

Scene: _____ Shot: _____ No. _____

Scene: _____ Shot: _____ No. _____

Scene: _____ Shot: _____ No. _____

Title: _____   Date: _____

Scene: _____   Shot: _____   No. _____

Scene: _____   Shot: _____   No. _____

Scene: _____   Shot: _____   No. _____

Scene: _____   Shot: _____   No. _____

Title: _____ Date: _____

Scene: _____ Shot: _____ No. _____

_____

_____

_____

_____

_____

_____

Scene: _____ Shot: _____ No. _____

_____

_____

_____

_____

_____

_____

_____

Scene: _____ Shot: _____ No. _____

_____

_____

_____

_____

_____

_____

Scene: _____ Shot: _____ No. _____

_____

_____

_____

_____

_____

_____

Title: _____ Date: _____

Scene:	Shot:	No.

Scene:	Shot:	No.

Scene:	Shot:	No.

Scene:	Shot:	No.

78

Title: _____   Date: _____

Scene:	Shot:	No.

Scene:	Shot:	No.

Scene:	Shot:	No.

Scene:	Shot:	No.

Title: _____   Date: _____

Scene:	Shot:	No.

_____

_____

_____

_____

_____

Scene:	Shot:	No.

_____

_____

_____

_____

_____

Scene:	Shot:	No.

_____

_____

_____

_____

_____

Scene:	Shot:	No.

_____

_____

_____

_____

_____

Title: _____   Date: _____

Scene: _____ Shot: _____ No. _____

Scene: _____ Shot: _____ No. _____

Scene: _____ Shot: _____ No. _____

Scene: _____ Shot: _____ No. _____

Title: _____   Date: _____

Scene:	Shot:	No.

Scene:	Shot:	No.

Scene:	Shot:	No.

Scene:	Shot:	No.

Title: _____   Date: _____

Scene:	Shot:	No.

Scene:	Shot:	No.

Scene:	Shot:	No.

Scene:	Shot:	No.

Title: _____   Date: _____

Scene:	Shot:	No.

Scene:	Shot:	No.

Scene:	Shot:	No.

Scene:	Shot:	No.

Title: _____   Date: _____

Scene: _____ Shot: _____ No. _____

Scene: _____ Shot: _____ No. _____

Scene: _____ Shot: _____ No. _____

Scene: _____ Shot: _____ No. _____

85

Title: _____   Date: _____

Scene:	Shot:	No.

Scene:	Shot:	No.

Scene:	Shot:	No.

Scene:	Shot:	No.

Title: _____   Date: _____

Scene: _____ Shot: _____ No. _____

_____

_____

_____

_____

_____

_____

Scene: _____ Shot: _____ No. _____

_____

_____

_____

_____

_____

_____

Scene: _____ Shot: _____ No. _____

_____

_____

_____

_____

_____

_____

Scene: _____ Shot: _____ No. _____

_____

_____

_____

_____

_____

_____

Title: _____   Date: _____

Scene:	Shot:	No.

Scene:	Shot:	No.

Scene:	Shot:	No.

Scene:	Shot:	No.

88

Title: _____   Date: _____

Scene: _____ Shot: _____ No. _____

Scene: _____ Shot: _____ No. _____

Scene: _____ Shot: _____ No. _____

Scene: _____ Shot: _____ No. _____

Title: _____   Date: _____

Scene:	Shot:	No.

Scene:	Shot:	No.

Scene:	Shot:	No.

Scene:	Shot:	No.

Title: _____   Date: _____

Scene:	Shot:	No.

Scene:	Shot:	No.

Scene:	Shot:	No.

Scene:	Shot:	No.

Title: _____   Date: _____

Scene:	Shot:	No.

Scene:	Shot:	No.

Scene:	Shot:	No.

Scene:	Shot:	No.

92

Title: _____   Date: _____

Scene: Shot: No.

Scene: Shot: No.

Scene: Shot: No.

Scene: Shot: No.

Title: _____   Date: _____

Scene:	Shot:	No.

_____
_____
_____
_____
_____

Scene:	Shot:	No.

_____
_____
_____
_____
_____

Scene:	Shot:	No.

_____
_____
_____
_____
_____

Scene:	Shot:	No.

_____
_____
_____
_____
_____

94

Title: _____   Date: _____

Scene: Shot: No.

Scene: Shot: No.

Scene: Shot: No.

Scene: Shot: No.

Title: _____   Date: _____

Scene: Shot: No.

Scene: Shot: No.

Scene: Shot: No.

Scene: Shot: No.

Title: _____   Date: _____

Scene:	Shot:	No.

Scene:	Shot:	No.

Scene:	Shot:	No.

Scene:	Shot:	No.

Title: _____   Date: _____

Scene:	Shot:	No.

Scene:	Shot:	No.

Scene:	Shot:	No.

Scene:	Shot:	No.

98

Title: _____   Date: _____

Scene: **Shot:**   **No.**

Scene: **Shot:**   **No.**

Scene: **Shot:**   **No.**

Scene: **Shot:**   **No.**

Title: _____   Date: _____

Scene:	Shot:	No.

Scene:	Shot:	No.

Scene:	Shot:	No.

Scene:	Shot:	No.

Title: _____   Date: _____

Scene: Shot: No.

Scene: Shot: No.

Scene: Shot: No.

Scene: Shot: No.

Title: _____   Date: _____

Scene:	Shot:	No.

Scene:	Shot:	No.

Scene:	Shot:	No.

Scene:	Shot:	No.

102

Title: _____   Date: _____

Scene: Shot: No.

Scene: Shot: No.

Scene: Shot: No.

Scene: Shot: No.

Title: _____   Date: _____

Scene:	Shot:	No.

Scene:	Shot:	No.

Scene:	Shot:	No.

Scene:	Shot:	No.

Title: _____   Date: _____

Scene:	Shot:	No.

Scene:	Shot:	No.

Scene:	Shot:	No.

Scene:	Shot:	No.

Title: _____   Date: _____

Scene: _____ Shot: _____ No. _____

Scene: _____ Shot: _____ No. _____

Scene: _____ Shot: _____ No. _____

Scene: _____ Shot: _____ No. _____

106

Title: _____   Date: _____

Scene: Shot: No.

Scene: Shot: No.

Scene: Shot: No.

Scene: Shot: No.

Title: _____   Date: _____

Scene: _____ Shot: _____ No. _____

_____

_____

_____

_____

_____

_____

Scene: _____ Shot: _____ No. _____

_____

_____

_____

_____

_____

_____

Scene: _____ Shot: _____ No. _____

_____

_____

_____

_____

_____

_____

Scene: _____ Shot: _____ No. _____

_____

_____

_____

_____

_____

_____

108

Title: _____   Date: _____

Scene: Shot: No.

Scene: Shot: No.

Scene: Shot: No.

Scene: Shot: No.

Title: _____   Date: _____

Scene: _____ Shot: _____ No. ____

Scene: _____ Shot: _____ No. ____

Scene: _____ Shot: _____ No. ____

Scene: _____ Shot: _____ No. ____

Title: _____   Date: _____

Scene:	Shot:	No.

Scene:	Shot:	No.

Scene:	Shot:	No.

Scene:	Shot:	No.

Title: _____   Date: _____

Scene: Shot: No.

Scene: Shot: No.

Scene: Shot: No.

Scene: Shot: No.

Title: _____   Date: _____

Scene:	Shot:	No.

_____

_____

_____

_____

_____

_____

Scene:	Shot:	No.

_____

_____

_____

_____

_____

_____

Scene:	Shot:	No.

_____

_____

_____

_____

_____

_____

Scene:	Shot:	No.

_____

_____

_____

_____

_____

_____

Title: _____   Date: _____

Scene: _____ Shot: _____ No. _____

Scene: _____ Shot: _____ No. _____

Scene: _____ Shot: _____ No. _____

Scene: _____ Shot: _____ No. _____

Title: _____   Date: _____

Scene:	Shot:	No.

Scene:	Shot:	No.

Scene:	Shot:	No.

Scene:	Shot:	No.

Title: _____   Date: _____

Scene: _____ Shot: _____ No. _____

Scene: _____ Shot: _____ No. _____

Scene: _____ Shot: _____ No. _____

Scene: _____ Shot: _____ No. _____

Title: _____   Date: _____

Scene:	Shot:	No.

Scene:	Shot:	No.

Scene:	Shot:	No.

Scene:	Shot:	No.

Title: _____ Date: _____

Scene:	Shot:	No.

Scene:	Shot:	No.

Scene:	Shot:	No.

Scene:	Shot:	No.

Title: _____   Date: _____

Scene:	Shot:	No.

Scene:	Shot:	No.

Scene:	Shot:	No.

Scene:	Shot:	No.

Title: _____   Date: _____

| Scene: | Shot: | No. |

_____

_____

_____

_____

_____

_____

| Scene: | Shot: | No. |

_____

_____

_____

_____

_____

| Scene: | Shot: | No. |

_____

_____

_____

_____

_____

_____

| Scene: | Shot: | No. |

_____

_____

_____

_____

_____

Title: _____   Date: _____

Scene:	Shot:	No.

Scene:	Shot:	No.

Scene:	Shot:	No.

Scene:	Shot:	No.

Title: _____ Date: _____

Scene: Shot: No.

Scene: Shot: No.

Scene: Shot: No.

Scene: Shot: No.

Title: _____   Date: _____

Scene: _____ Shot: _____ No. _____

_____
_____
_____
_____
_____
_____

Scene: _____ Shot: _____ No. _____

_____
_____
_____
_____
_____
_____
_____

Scene: _____ Shot: _____ No. _____

_____
_____
_____
_____
_____
_____
_____

Scene: _____ Shot: _____ No. _____

_____
_____
_____
_____
_____
_____

3707444R00070

Made in the USA
Middletown, DE
19 November 2016